Highland Cattle

by Julie Murray

FANCY FARM ANIMALS

Abdo Kids Jumbo is an Imprint of Abdo Kids
abdobooks.com

abdobooks.com

Published by Abdo Kids, a division of ABDO, P.O. Box 398166, Minneapolis, Minnesota 55439. Copyright © 2026 by Abdo Consulting Group, Inc. International copyrights reserved in all countries. No part of this book may be reproduced in any form without written permission from the publisher. Abdo Kids Jumbo™ is a trademark and logo of Abdo Kids.

Printed in the United States of America, North Mankato, Minnesota.

052025

092025

Photo Credits: Alamy, Getty Images, Shutterstock

Production Contributors: Teddy Borth, Jennie Forsberg, Grace Hansen
Design Contributors: Candice Keimig, Pakou Moua

Library of Congress Control Number: 2024947608
Publisher's Cataloging-in-Publication Data

Names: Murray, Julie, author.

Title: Highland cattle / by Julie Murray

Description: Minneapolis, Minnesota : Abdo Kids, 2026 | Series: Fancy farm animals | Includes online resources and index.

Identifiers: ISBN 9798384905233 (lib. bdg.) | ISBN 9798384905936 (ebook) | ISBN 9798384906285 (Read-to-me ebook)

Subjects: LCSH: Highland cattle--Juvenile literature. | Cattle--Juvenile literature. | Farm animals--Juvenile literature. | Livestock--Juvenile literature. | Domestic animals--Juvenile literature.

Classification: DDC 636.2--dc23

Table of Contents

Highland Cattle 4	More Facts 22
Body 12	Glossary 23
Diet 18	Index 24
Baby Highland Cattle 20	Abdo Kids Code. 24

Highland Cattle

Highland cattle are known for their shaggy hair and gentle personalities. They enjoy the company of both humans and their herd. They are popular fancy farm animals!

Highland cattle are one of the oldest cattle **breeds**. They have been around since the 6th century! They come from the Scottish Highlands and the Western Isles of Scotland.

Today, there are no Highland cattle in the wild. They are found on farms and ranches around the world. Some are even kept as pets.

Highland cattle are mainly raised for their meat. Some **hobbyists** raise cattle for show. The cattle are judged on things such as their body, hair, head, and horns.

Body

Highland cattle are large cows. Males stand nearly 4 feet (1.2 m) at the shoulders. They can weigh more than 1,800 pounds (816.5 kg)! Females are smaller than males.

Highland cattle are strong animals with a **broad** chest. Their legs are short and powerful. Their tail is long. Their horns curve upward.

Highland cattle have long, shaggy hair. Red is the most common color. Some cattle are black, white, or yellow in color. The fringe that grows over the cow's eyes is called a dossan. It protects the eyes.

Diet

Highland cattle spend 8 hours a day **grazing**. They eat grass, leaves, shrubs, and hay. They eat up to 150 pounds (68 kg) of food each day!

Baby Highland Cattle

Female highland cattle usually give birth to one calf. The calf is 60 pounds (27.2 kg) at birth. It will be fully grown when it is 5 years old.

More Facts

- Male Highland cattle are called bulls. Females are called cows. A group of Highland cattle is called a herd or fold. The Scots sometimes refer to them as "Hairy Coos."

- Highland cattle are **hardy** animals that can survive in harsh weather.

- Highland cattle use their horns to defend themselves from **predators**. They also use their horns to dig through the snow to find food.

Glossary

breed – a group of animals usually found only under human care and different from related kinds.

broad – wide or large.

grazing – feeding on growing grass.

hardy – able to stand or live through harsh weather or bad conditions.

hobbyist – a person who does an activity for pleasure in their spare time.

predator – an animal that hunts other animals for food.

Index

babies 20

chest 14

color 16

eyes 16

food 18

hair 4, 10, 16

head 10

horns 10, 14

legs 14

personality 4

Scottish Highlands 6

size 12, 20

tail 14

uses 8, 10

Western Isles 6

Visit **abdokids.com** to access crafts, games, videos, and more!

Use Abdo Kids code **FHK5233** or scan this QR code!